Deleted

Deleted

NATURAL PHENOMENA

TIDES

by Lisa Bullard

FOCUS READERS

WWW.FOCUSREADERS.COM

Focus Readers is distributed by North Star Editions:
sales@northstareditions.com | 888-417-0195

Produced for Focus Readers by Red Line Editorial.

Content Consultant: Dr. David A. Brooks, Professor of Oceanography, Texas A&M University

Photographs ©: forestpath/Shutterstock Images, cover, 1; Denise Lett/Shutterstock Images, 4–5; Stephen Rees/Shutterstock Images, 7; CL-Medien/Shutterstock Images, 9; Johan Swanepoel/Shutterstock Images, 10–11; fluidworkshop/Shutterstock Images, 12, 19; Frank L Junior/Shutterstock Images, 14; Adam Springer/Shutterstock Images, 16–17; B V Nickel/Shutterstock Images, 20; Wang Chaoying/Imaginechina/AP Images, 23; James Wheeler/Shutterstock Images, 24–25; Ethan Daniels/Shutterstock Images, 26; Watchares Hansawek/Shutterstock Images, 29

ISBN
978-1-63517-913-2 (hardcover)
978-1-64185-015-5 (paperback)
978-1-64185-217-3 (ebook pdf)
978-1-64185-116-9 (hosted ebook)

Library of Congress Control Number: 2018931706

Printed in the United States of America
Mankato, MN
May, 2018

ABOUT THE AUTHOR

Lisa Bullard is the author of more than 90 books for children, including the mystery novel *Turn Left at the Cow*. She also teaches writing classes for adults and children. Lisa grew up in Minnesota and now lives just north of Minneapolis.

TABLE OF CONTENTS

CHAPTER 1

THE CHANGING TIDE

Muddy sand stretches to the ocean. The sunny beach seems peaceful. But there's a battle taking place. It's a struggle between land and sea. For now, the water appears to be winning. It moves up the shore, swallowing more and more of the beach. Finally, the beach is completely covered by water.

The tide moves up toward the rocks on the coast of California.

But this fight isn't over. At just past the six-hour mark, the water holds still. Then the ocean begins to pull away. It loses ground to the land. A little more than 12 hours after it began its advance, the water has gone into full retreat. It no longer covers the beach. The exposed mud dries in the cooling night. Then the process starts all over. The water begins creeping back up the shore.

This regular rise and fall of the ocean surface is known as the tide. As the water level rises and falls, it creates **currents** in the water. A flood current moves inland with a rising tide. It washes up over the shoreline. Over the next few hours, the

A flood current rushes in at Porthminster Beach in Cornwall, England.

tide falls. The water moves back out. This is an ebb current.

Most coastal areas have two high tides and two low tides each day. The water rises to high tide in slightly more than six hours. Then it falls back to low tide.

This process takes a little more than six hours as well. The time for high and low tides changes each day. But the tide keeps repeating the same pattern. It goes from low tide to high tide and back again. The land that is covered by water at high tide and dry at low tide is known as the intertidal zone.

TIDAL RANGE

The tidal range is the height difference between high and low tides. Along some coasts, the tidal range is only a few inches. But in many locations, the change is much greater. Canada's Bay of Fundy is one example. The tidal range there can reach more than 50 feet (16 m).

The Bay of Fundy's rock formations are exposed during low tide.

CHAPTER 2

WHAT CAUSES TIDES?

Tides happen because of Earth's relationship to the moon. **Gravity** is a force that pulls the moon and Earth toward each other. This force causes the moon to orbit in a curve around Earth. But gravity works against **inertia**. Inertia tries to make the moon and Earth move in straight lines.

The moon takes approximately 27 days to make a complete orbit of Earth.

It's as if gravity and inertia are playing tug-of-war. On the side of Earth that is closest to the moon, gravity wins. It pulls ocean waters toward the moon.

TIDAL BULGES

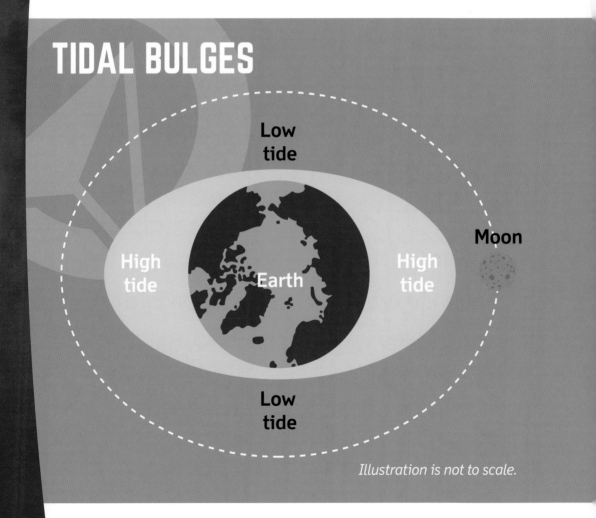

Low tide

High tide

Earth

High tide

Moon

Low tide

Illustration is not to scale.

This makes the waters bulge. A high tide happens.

On the side farthest from the moon, inertia wins. This creates a bulge away from the moon. High tide happens on this side as well. So, at any given time, there are two high tides on opposite sides of Earth. The two sides in between have low tides.

The part of Earth that is closest to the moon is always changing. As Earth rotates, each point on its surface passes under the two bulges and the two lows. It changes from high tide to low tide and back again. Earth makes one complete turn every 24 hours. This is a solar day.

High tide rushes over rocks in Ecola State Park along the coast of Oregon.

Meanwhile, the moon is moving in the same direction as Earth is turning. As a result, it takes approximately 24 hours and 50 minutes for each point on Earth's surface to rotate back to be closest to the moon. This period of time is called a lunar day. A lunar day is longer than 24 hours, so tides happen approximately 50 minutes later each day.

The sun also affects tides. The sun is much bigger than the moon. But it is much farther from Earth. This distance makes the sun's impact on tides smaller. Its impact is about half of the moon's.

ANCIENT TIDE THEORIES

Our understanding of the tide comes from modern science. But long ago, people had other theories. The Mayans said tides were caused by a giant crab moving in the water. The ancient Greek philosopher Plato thought Earth was a large animal. He believed the tides were fluids moving inside it.

CHAPTER 3

WHY TIDES DIFFER

The tide can be very different from one location to the next. The shape of the shoreline is an important factor. If the shore is smooth and flat, the water can spread out. The tide may not rise much. In other places, the coast is a narrow, rocky bay. The water is trapped inside. Here, the tide may rise many feet.

The tide may reach high up a shore that has steep, rocky cliffs.

Even in one place, the tide can vary. Twice each **lunar month**, the sun, the moon, and Earth closely line up. At these times, the moon's gravity and the sun's gravity work together. They create the biggest difference between high and low tides. These are called spring tides.

At two other times each month, the sun and the moon are almost at **right angles** to each other. The tidal bulges caused by the sun almost line up with the tidal lows caused by the moon. The bulges and lows partly cancel each other out. As a result, there is the smallest difference between high tides and low tides. These smaller tides are called neap tides.

THE SUN, MOON, AND TIDES

SPRING TIDE

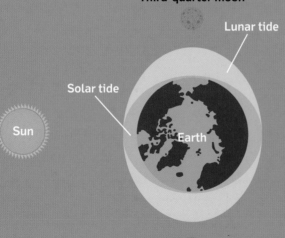

Lunar tide

Solar tide

Full
moon

New
moon

Sun

Earth

NEAP TIDE

Third-quarter moon

Lunar tide

Solar tide

Sun

Earth

First-quarter moon

Illustration is not to scale.

Some places along the Gulf of Mexico have diurnal tides, or only one high tide and one low tide each day.

Some places experience unequal high tides every day. They may also have unequal low tides. This difference is caused by the moon's orbit around Earth. The moon's orbit looks like an ellipse, or oval. This orbit is tilted compared to Earth's **equator**. Therefore, the distance between places on Earth and the tidal bulges can vary. They are closer together during one high tide. This tide is larger.

In some places, the difference is so big that there is only one high tide each day. These places have only one low tide as well. This strange pattern can also be caused by the shape of the coast.

FORECASTING THE TIDE

Tide tables show the expected times and heights of local tides. The earliest known tide table is from China in the year 1056. In the 1800s, people began using machines to forecast the tide. Today, computers do this job. Tide tables are posted online for locations around the world. But forecasting the tide is complicated. Many things can alter the forecast.

TIDAL BORES

A tidal bore is a large wave that moves upstream in a shallow river or narrow **inlet**. This unusual event is caused by the incoming tide. The shallow water slows down the tide wave. As the wave slows, water piles up at the front.

Tidal bores happen in just a few dozen places around the world. For instance, the mouth of the Amazon River in Brazil is famous for its tidal bores. So is the Turnagain Arm. This narrow channel is in Alaska. In all these locations, rivers or inlets empty into an ocean. These places usually have large tidal ranges as well.

The world's largest tidal bore races up the Qiantang River in China. This tidal bore is usually at its highest at the mid-autumn full moon. Crowds gather every year to watch the amazing sight. Surfers are also drawn to tidal bore locations. Surfing a regular ocean wave lasts for

A tidal bore rushes down the Qiantang River.

only a few seconds. But tidal bores give surfers the chance to ride a single wave for miles.

CHAPTER 4

ALONG THE SHORE

Many plants and animals live in the intertidal zone. Scientists divide it into four smaller zones. The splash zone is the highest up. It is never underwater. Spray reaches it only during high tide. Animals in this zone must be able to live out of water. Barnacles, seals, and sea otters can be found here.

The intertidal zone is home to many kinds of wildlife.

Starfish often live in tide pools.

The high-tide zone is covered in water at high tide. Animals and plants here are hit by strong waves. Many have tough shells and cling to rocks. If they don't hold on tight, water will sweep them out to sea. Mussels and crabs often live in this zone.

Tide pools are typically found in the mid-zone. This zone is exposed during low tide. But tide pools catch and hold water. Wildlife inside them stays wet even when the tide goes out. Animals in tide pools tend to have shells. But many have soft bodies. Snails, hermit crabs, and sea anemones are common.

AT THE BOTTOM

In some places, the intertidal zone has a rocky bottom. In other places, the bottom is soft. Animals hide in sand or silt during low tide so they do not dry out. They come out to eat during high tide. High tide brings food from deeper water. But it also brings large fish that might eat the animals.

The last zone is the low-tide zone. It is usually underwater. But it is dry during low tide. People often come to the shore during low tide to fish or gather shellfish.

Tides affect people, too. Large numbers of people live near the ocean. And many major cities are on coasts. Bridges and buildings must be built with the changing water levels in mind.

Sailors must understand the time and height of tides. They must know the speed and direction of the currents. In the past, sailing ships used these currents to move. Most ships no longer use sails. But many **cargo** ships are huge. Water levels must be just right for them to navigate

People collect crabs during low tide.

shallow waters near the coast. If the water is too low, a ship may get stuck. Its cargo may go bad before high tide returns. Or, if the water is too high, the ship may not fit under a bridge. These are just some of the many ways tides affect life along the coast. People will continue to study them for many years to come.

FOCUS ON
TIDES

Write your answers on a separate piece of paper.

1. Write a paragraph that describes three ways the tide affects people.

2. Would you want to surf a tidal bore? Why or why not?

3. Which part of the intertidal zone is never completely covered in water?

    A. the mid-zone
    B. the high-tide zone
    C. the splash zone

4. How are animals in the high-tide zone and the mid-zone similar?

    A. Both have very hard bodies.
    B. Both tend to have protective shells.
    C. Both can only survive underwater.

Answer key on page 32.

GLOSSARY

cargo
Items carried by a vehicle from one place to another.

currents
Water movements that go in a certain direction.

equator
An imaginary line that runs around the middle of Earth.

gravity
The force one object has on another due to the mass of each object and how far apart they are.

inertia
The tendency of an object to keep doing what it is already doing.

inlet
A thin body of water that reaches into land from a large body of water, such as an ocean.

lunar month
The period of time between two new moons, or approximately 29 days.

right angles
Angles that measure 90 degrees, such as the corners of a square.

TO LEARN MORE

BOOKS

Haelle, Tara. *Seasons, Tides, and Lunar Phases*. Vero
  Beach, FL: Rourke Educational Media, 2016.
Parker, Steve. *In Focus: Oceans and Seas*. New York:
  Kingfisher, 2017.
Rooney, Anne. *You Wouldn't Want to Live without Gravity!*
  New York: Scholastic, 2016.
Woodward, John. *Ocean: A Visual Encyclopedia*. New York:
  DK Publishing, 2015.

NOTE TO EDUCATORS

Visit **www.focusreaders.com** to find lesson plans,
activities, links, and other resources related to this title.

INDEX

Answer Key: 1. Answers will vary; **2.** Answers will vary; **3.** C; **4.** B